CRAPCARS

CRAPCARS

RICHARD PORTER

BLOOMSBURY

Published by Bloomsbury Publishing, New York and London
Distributed to the trade by Holtzbrinck Publishers

All papers used by Bloomsbury Publishing are natural, recyclable products made from wood grown in well-managed forests.
The manufacturing processes conform to the environmental regulations of the country of origin.

The author would like to thank Brett Berk for his tireless research, without which this book would be as crap as the cars in it.

Library of Congress Cataloging-in-Publication Data

Porter, Richard, 1975–
Crap Cars / Richard Porter.—1st U.S. ed.
p. cm.
ISBN 1-58234-638-0 (hardcover)
ISBN-13 978-1-58234-638-0
1. Automobiles. I. Title.

TL147.P66 2005
629.222—dc22
2004026344

First U.S. Edition 2005

1 3 5 7 9 10 8 6 4 2

Designed by Elizabeth Van Itallie
Printed in China

CONTENTS

INTRODUCTION

When it came to picking the fifty unsavory subjects for this book, frankly, we were spoiled for choice. It was like gorging on the biggest buffet you've ever seen, and just as likely to make you puke. Some people won't like all the choices; that's probably because they've got one of them parked outside and there's still a year left on the payments. Other people will be the kind of nitpickers who are going to claim that in a specific year or with a certain option package one of these cars actually touched on the fringes of acceptability. Well, we've thought of that, which is why we've tried to be as clear as possible about particular model names, production years, and so on. If you're either of these types of people, we apologize in advance for any offense caused or any mistakes made. On the other hand, maybe you should get out more. For the rest of you, enjoy the book. Unless you designed any of the cars in it. In which case, we hope it gives you a paper cut.

50

IF THIS CAR WAS...
A REAL PORSCHE,
MICHAEL JACKSON IS A
REAL WHITE GUY.

PORSCHE 924 (1976–1985)

Here's a phrase you never want to hear: Low-performance Porsche. The feeble 924's life started when Volkswagen asked Porsche to design a coupe for them. Then Volkswagen, having emptied out all their pockets, been through their spare jacket, and pulled all the cushions off the sofa, realized they didn't have the cash to pay for it and beat a red-faced retreat. However, since the car was pretty much ready, Porsche simply slapped their own badge on it and put it on sale without even changing the Volkswagen engine for one of their own. Which was an error because the motor was from a VW van. Doh! Unsurprisingly, the engine was utterly pathetic and imbued the 924 with all the get up and go of an octogenarian in lead shoes. A while later Porsche pulled up their lederhosen and fitted one of their own engines, but until then the 924 was as pointless as teaching a horse to play tennis.

BMW 318i [1984]

It's the eternal problem with BMWs: no one can deny most of their cars are engineering masterpieces, yet everyone will assume you're a pushy Yuppie jerk for driving one. And what better way to confirm that suspicion than by buying one of the few BMWs that wasn't an object of technical brilliance and, as a result, also wasn't even fast enough to leave them eating your stockbroker-scented exhaust fumes? BMW may have made its name with smooth, powerful six-cylinder engines, but don't expect one under the hood of an '84 318i. Instead there was a bandy-legged four-cylinder with all the rippling power of a newborn giraffe. And just to complete the tragedy, they had the nerve to jack up the price so that it cost twice as much as the previous 320. What's the German for "bamboozled" anyway?

IF THIS CAR WAS . . .
ANY MORE OF A CON, THEY'D PUT IT IN JAIL.

IF THIS CAR WAS...
BETTER LOOKING, IT MIGHT
HAVE BEEN QUITE NICE.

JAGUAR XJS-C (1988)

The main problem with turning a sports coupe into a convertible is that without a roof to hold it together, the whole car will become as rigid as a Jell-O ladder. The best way to solve this problem is to carefully engineer a series of subtle body-shell reinforcements to restore some of the strength without anyone noticing. Or, in Jaguar's case, you could simply weld a pile of scaffolding to the top of the car, jam a pair of targa panels above the passengers' heads, and fill in the hole behind them with a big canvas flap. Job done, chaps, let's all go to the pub. Except it wasn't job well done at all because it turned the once sleek XJS into a total disaster with all the visual appeal of a baboon in party dress.

CADILLAC ETC (2000-2002)

Here's a great example of the marketing department really spoiling things. The Cadillac Etcetera? What kind of lame-ass name is that? Good thing those same genii weren't let loose on other products, or we'd all be buying Apple iWhatevers, chewing on Wrigley's Yadda Yadda Yadda, and being sold Coors, "the only beer with, like, y'know, some stuff in it." Of course, marketing can't take all the blame for this crap Caddy; someone should have fired the stylists too, because the last time something sported pillars that thick it stood on a mountain above Athens. The Etcetera is possibly the only car that should have come imprinted with the words "Objects in the rearview mirror may be completely invisible behind all that bodywork."

IF THIS CAR WAS...
MERGING ONTO A FREEWAY,
THERE ISN'T A CHANCE IN HELL
IT WOULD SEE YOU.

IF THIS CAR WAS...
A MOVIE, IT WOULD BE
"LOST IN TRANSLATION."

MERKUR SCORPIO (1987–1989)

Coming straight out of the Long-Forgotten File, the Merkur was a European Ford, inexplicably adapted for sale in the United States. Back in its homeland, this was a large car and pretty radical in a blobby sort of way. But transplanted to a place where gas doesn't cost more than liquid platinum, the Scorp made rather less sense. In fact, it made no sense at all. Unsurprisingly, sales were pathetic until Ford decided to stop being so silly. They deleted the Scorpio from American price lists, and then killed the entire Merkur brand, just to be safe. In fairness, this car was reasonably popular in Germany. But so is oompah music.

VOLVO 262C (1977-1981)

One of the greatest things about mankind is our constantly inquiring minds—minds that led us to conquer continents, explore space, and invent a way to electrically clip nose hair. But there are some questions that don't need answering. Questions such as "I wonder if I could drop this glockenspiel on my own head?," or "What would happen if I lived entirely on potato chips?," or, worst of all, "What would happen if you sliced the roof off a Volvo sedan and replaced it with what appears to be the top of a mid-70s pimp-mobile?" Well, here's your answer—it would look ridiculous. But that didn't stop them making it.

IF THIS CAR WAS...
IN YOUR DREAMS,
THEY'D CHANGE
YOUR MEDICATION.

44

**IF THIS CAR WAS...
SUCH A GOOD IDEA,
WHY'D THEY STOP
MAKING IT?**

NISSAN NX (1991–1993)

Sometimes the strangest things can seem like a good idea. Ironing your clothes while wearing them, for example. Perhaps putting your breakfast, lunch, and dinner into a blender and drinking it all at once. Or, for that matter, buying a car with interchangeable rear ends so that you could switch between driving a sedan and a small wagon. But if you think about it, they're not good ideas at all. In fact, they're completely stupid. Especially the car.

GM EV1 (1996-1999)

Every so often GM stops being lazy and predictable and actually tries hard to do something different. Unfortunately this is normally a guarantee of an epic mistake on the horizon. Bingo! The EV1, GM's honest attempt to make the world's first electric car. Designed to appeal to the world's first car buyers who only ever wanted to go a few miles from their house. And just so your neighbors knew you were doing your bit to save the planet, they gave it a distinctive body that looked like a snake trapped under a rock.

IF THIS CAR WAS...
BLESSED WITH ANY LESS RANGE, THEY MIGHT AS WELL HAVE LEFT IT PLUGGED IN.

42

JAGUAR XJ6 (1987–1994)

When the XJ6 was announced in 1986 it was described as a "clean sheet design." In which case Jaguar had clearly taken that clean sheet, written on it everything that people loved about their cars, and then thrown it in the trash. Good-bye to curvaceous styling, strong performance, and traditionally luxurious interiors, hello to the box-fronted horror you see here with its appalling Atari-like dashboard and all the acceleration of a tired snail. Still, there were at least two "traditional" Jaguar qualities that remained: the one that made various major components work on a strictly part-time basis and the one that allowed sundry pieces of the interior to fall off. In fairness to Jaguar, the XJ6 was developed on the kind of budget that BMW would allocate to a new ashtray, which perhaps explains why, once they'd carved the finished design out of clay and sent it away to be turned into metal, the back end melted, giving it an unintentionally saggy appearance that nobody bothered to fix. This was probably the greatest travesty of all. Because no one expects the back of a Jag to look like the buttocks of a plumber poking over the top of his slack-assed jeans.

OLDSMOBILE TORONADO TROFEO (1989)

God bless General Motors and its amazing ability to shuttle wildly between technology that was either stubbornly old-fashioned or inadvisably advanced. This, in case you're wondering, is one from the inadvisable file. Specifically, we're talking about the nightmarish future world that was predicted by the introduction of a touch-screen on-board computer, which GM charmingly called VIC, or Visual Information Center. Forget your boring conventional dashboard controls, because this little baby would take care of your in-car entertainment and air conditioning settings, as well as giving you information such as the time and the fuel consumption plus a whole crazy vista of additional features including something called a "date book." Of course, it's safe to say that you're much less likely to get an actual date if you spend all your time outside playing with the stupid computer in your car. If VIC was meant to be a precursor of the near future then the 1990s would have been a time of needless complexity, garish graphics, and the endless smear of fingerprints. In fact, all you need to know about VIC is that one reviewer strongly advised any keen Trofeo buyer to seek out an example that *didn't* have this system.

IF THIS CAR WAS...
TO GET ITS OWN COMPUTER TO WRITE THIS BIT, IT WOULD SAY: ;BQA43R;OUJ\SD'AK,F.

40

**IF THIS CAR WAS...
AN ACTUAL HORSE,
YOU'D SHOOT IT.**

FERRARI 400 (1976-1979)

It doesn't take a genius to explain that the two things you should expect from any Ferrari are performance and beauty. Unfortunately Ferrari themselves completely forgot about that when they designed this monster. With a 4.8-liter V12 engine up front you might have vainly hoped that this car would be quick, but it wasn't, especially when hooked up to a smothering automatic gearbox. Couple this with graceless cornering and disturbingly feeble brakes and you had a real recipe for misery. Expensive, handmade misery, but misery nonetheless. In any other Ferrari you might have consoled yourself by slipping down to the garage and simply drinking in its smooth, sinuous curves, but not with this horror. Not unless you got really excited by large-scale origami. A sobering reminder that the intern is there to make coffee and photocopy stuff, not to design a whole car.

STERLING 825/827 (1987-1991)

It seemed like such a good idea. Rover of Britain and Honda of Japan would join forces to make a luxury car. The Japanese would bring the build quality, reliability, and precision engineering. The British would garnish it with their talent for suspension tuning and tasteful design. Both companies were so excited about the prospect of wooing the American market that each invented a whole new brand with which to sell their brilliant new car; Acura for Honda's version, Sterling for Rover's. What could possibly go wrong? For Acura, nothing. For Sterling? Absolutely everything. Maybe if they'd listened to Honda's suggestions on, for example, how to make the doors fit properly they would have ended up with a good car. But they didn't, so they didn't. Instead the Sterling was a shabby festival of lame quality, including a dashboard that turned green in strong sunlight, and it was marketed with all the competence of the Three Stooges let loose in an ad agency. In fact, the only bit of the Sterling that was even remotely dependable was the engine. And—surprise, surprise—that came from Honda.

**IF THIS CAR WAS...
TRYING ANY HARDER
TO BE BRITISH,
IT'D BE MADONNA.**

38

ROLLS-ROYCE
CAMARGUE (1975–1986)

In the 1970s Rolls-Royce decided to break with tradition by getting respected Italian design studio Pininfarina to create a stylish body for its new coupe. Unfortunately it looks like there was some sort of mixup and the job was actually given to Gianni Pininfarina, a plumber from Milan, who knew nothing whatsoever about car design. As a result the Camargue looked utterly terrible, not least because the entire body appeared too big for the wheels, making it unpleasantly reminiscent of a fat man sitting on a bar stool. It's also worth noting that there was some huffing, puffing, and high-frequency mustache twitching among hard-core Rolls-Royce fans because those damned Italians had dared to give the company's famous radiator grille a slight rearward

slant. Obviously this rather overlooked the more pressing point that even if you tilt a hog's nose back a couple of degrees, it's still a big fat pig.

DELOREAN DMC-12 (1981–1983)

John Z. DeLorean spent much of the 1960s and early 1970s working for GM, where he created cars such as the legendary Pontiac GTO. That's the sort of cool stuff you get to do when you're a handsome cowboy figure and your middle name starts with a Z. The trouble started when John Z. got sick of working for The Man and decided to create his own "ethical" sports car. Originally his "ethics" revolved around environmental friendliness, although this soon gave way to the rather less ethical business of persuading the British government to give him enormous bags of cash so he could set up a brand-new factory in Northern Ireland. The end result was, frankly, dismal. Sure that stainless steel body looked good, at least until it got covered in fingerprints, but the build quality was appalling and that 2.8-liter V6 engine was so weak it would struggle to pull a hobo off your sister. DMC-12 sales were dismal, falling rapidly to zero when John Z. got caught in a doomed money laundering sting and had to shut his car factory forever. The car did rise again as the star of the movie *Back to the Future*, although even in 1955 they'd probably have noticed it was a broken promise.

IF THIS CAR WAS…
A REAL TIME MACHINE,
MAYBE THE BRITISH GOVERNMENT
COULD GO GET
THEIR MONEY BACK.

36

IF THIS CAR WAS...
WEATHER, IT WOULD
BE DRIZZLE.

AMC/RENAULT
ALLIANCE (1983-1988)

When Renault decided to join forces with a domestic manufacturer in order to increase their sales across America they could barely have chosen a worse partner than AMC. Unless of course they wanted to pick the only automaker whose own products made Renaults look attractive. In which case, job done. The Alliance set the tone for the new partnership and that tone can only be described as underwhelming. In fact this was a car of such crushing dismalness and feeble construction that it made you want to walk to work, even if your office was seventy miles away. In Europe, where the Alliance was sold as the Renault 9, it inexplicably won the Car of the Year award, which just goes to show that if people can't agree on the candidate they like, the winner will be the one that no one likes at all.

CHRYSLER IMPERIAL (1990)

The Imperial was based on the K-car, which, as bad starts go, is up there with being the offspring of Tom Arnold. To cover the embarrassing parentage Chrysler had to disguise it, apparently by asking everyone in the company for styling suggestions. And then they used them. All of them. Covered headlights? Yep! Chrome mirrors? Okay! Chrome window surrounds? Sure! Yet more strips of chrome stuck to the fenders and door handles and taillights and all over the car as if it had been attacked by a toddler with an electrolysis kit? You got it! And then, to cap it all, they gave it an opera roof. Wow! Welcome to the 1990s. Same as it ever was—crap.

**IF THIS CAR WAS...
ANY MORE OVERDESIGNED,
IT WOULD COLLAPSE.**

IF THIS CAR WAS... SOLD WITHOUT A STEERING WHEEL, IT COULD BARELY HAVE BEEN LESS ERRATIC.

MASERATI BITURBO (1984–1994)

Mmm, *Maserati*. Doesn't the very mention of its name make you think of swishing across Europe in a cool sixties coupe, en route to a rendezvous in a Monte Carlo casino where you'll win the money, shoot the baddies, and get the girl? Then you see this—the Biturbo. Old Maseratis were called exotic things such as Mistral, Khamsin, and Kyalami, so what sort of tediously functional name was *Biturbo*? And what sort of tediously functional design was it pinned to? Maseratis were meant to be ruthlessly rakish, not stubby and square. Who wants to swish to the South of France in something that looks like a child's drawing of a car? Mind you, given build quality best described as approximate, you'd count yourself lucky even to reach the Alps before something went catastrophically wrong. Which would at least spare you the embarrassment of arriving in Monaco in a really crap Maserati.

TRIUMPH TR7 (1975-1981)

The 1970s weren't a good time for British sports car makers. Without fail their products were as fresh as month-old milk, and proposed new safety regulations threatened to keep them from American soil forever. Triumph had a solution. They would design—shock!—a brand-new car, and one that would meet anything the federal legislators could throw at it. Unfortunately someone must have mis-read the projected plans for rollover protection and assumed that, if the car did flip over, the roof must be so ugly that the ground would actually attempt to repel it. Legend has it that upon first encountering a TR7, Italian car design guru Giorgetto Giugiaro drank in the strange creases up the flanks, walked slowly halfway around the car, and exclaimed, "My God! They've done it to the other side as well!" History doesn't record his next utterance but I like to think it was, "Get it away, get it away! Arrrgh! My eyes!"

IF THIS CAR WAS...
A "TRIUMPH," IMAGINE
WHAT A FAILURE
WOULD LOOK LIKE.

NISSAN 300ZX (1984–1989)

The Datsun Z-car used to be a hip young gunslinger, a laid-back coupe that took the thrusting looks of a muscle car and mixed them with the precision engineering and relentless reliability of a Japanese econo-box. People loved 'em, and rightly so. But all good things must come to an end, and this was one of the most dismal ends ever. Compared to the glory days of the original 240Z, the 300ZX was slow and wheezy and had all the vigor of a lazy koala. It was a hopeless car, seemingly designed for sweaty Houston dentists and their blubber-butt golf club buddies. Starting off lithe and sexy and ending up so lardy and useless, never before had a car so spectacularly "done an Elvis."

IF THIS CAR WAS...
ANY PORKIER,
YOU'D ROAST IT.

ASTON MARTIN
LAGONDA (1976–1985)

In the mid-1970s Aston Martin was in trouble. Thanks to the fuel crisis, lavish British sports cars were not at the top of most people's shopping lists and the company was broke. This left them with a choice: either they could batten down the hatches and weather the storm, remembering that they'd survived worse in the past, or they could take out their trusty service revolver and shoot themselves squarely in the foot. They chose the second option. Yes, Aston Martin decided that their best course of action was to go crazy and design a large luxury sedan packed with zany, car-of-the-future technology such as digital instruments and, on early models, touch-sensitive buttons instead of a gearshift, neither of which stood any chance of working properly. Little wonder that this car was popular only in the Middle East, where they had lots of money to pay for the Lagonda's massive repair bills and, when they'd had enough of that, lots of desert in which to bury it.

IF THIS CAR WAS…
ANY MORE ANGULAR,
IT'D HAVE SQUARE WHEELS.

IF THIS CAR WAS... ANY WEIRDER, THEY'D PUT IT IN THE NUTHOUSE.

SUBARU XT (1985-1991)

Four-wheel drive is, by and large, a good thing. In SUVs it's often switched on all the time, to haul you out of muddy ruts. In sports cars it only works when you need it, to improve grip on slippery corners. But what about the Subaru XT? Plainly this wasn't an SUV nor, despite the stupidly pointy coupe styling, was it a sports car. So what sort of four-wheel-drive system would it have? Permanent? Part time? Or one that only worked when you *switched on the windshield wipers*? Sadly, it was the third one. There was more strangeness in the steering wheel—which was asymmetrical for no good reason at all—and the weird gearstick—which was plainly meant to look like a jet fighter's joystick but actually resembled a big phallus. And, as luck would have it, that's how you'd feel if you were driving one.

CHRYSLER TC
BY MASERATI (1989-1991)

When Chrysler bought a stake in Italian supercar maker Maserati they were conned, because the cars Maserati made at that moment were anything but super. Thus, Maserati weren't really in a position to help with this miserable vehicle, aside from providing some cheap badges to stick on the front. Thankfully Chrysler was more than capable of coming up with an overpriced Le Baron with a porthole window on their own, thanks very much. Best of all was an advertisement for the TC that claimed that this crock was "built and handcrafted." Built and handcrafted? So they bolted it all together, and then added the handcrafted bits? "Handcrafted" in this context clearly meaning the wonky trim, the nasty plastics, the overall feeling that you'd just been sold a lightly polished piece of poop. And just look at those seats. Ever wondered what it'd be like to see your grandparents naked?

IF THIS CAR WAS...
A REAL MASERATI,
IT WOULD HAVE BEEN
EVEN MORE BADLY MADE.

28

FORD EXP (1982)

What an odd time the eighties were. Big hair, shoulder pads, a career for Kelly LeBrock. And weirdest of all, this—yes, *this*—was sold as a sports car. Except of course the EXP wasn't anything like a sports car, mainly because it was based on the Escort. Other Ford projects around the same time probably included a sneaker based on a combat boot. Sure, they tried pretty hard with the EXP's Star Wars styling and its enigmatic name—"Want *your* product to sound slightly futuristic? Use an X! The letter that's slightly futuristic!"—but no one was fooled for long. It was an Escort in a Darth Vader suit, no more, no less. Thankfully, the EXP is an eighties creation we no longer have to put up with, just like big hair and shoulder pads. Kelly LeBrock, on the other hand, is always welcome back.

HUMMER H1 (1993-2002)

Imagine if there'd been some sort of hideous Pentagon mess-up and someone had decided that the army would go into battle driving a fleet of Camrys. It would be stupid, everyone would laugh, somewhere down the line people would probably get injured. So why in the name of all that's holy is it somehow acceptable to cruise down to the mall in a military vehicle? It's not difficult to see why drivers might find a big SUV appealing, but sometimes things can be too big. And that time is when your SUV is so massive that you won't even notice if you drive over something smaller. Like New York City. You know who the Hummer's biggest fan is? Arnold Schwarzenegger. Need I say more?

IF THIS CAR WAS...
ANY BIGGER, YOU COULD
SEE IT FROM SPACE.

IF THIS CAR WAS...
SPORTY, GÉRARD
DEPARDIEU IS A PINUP.

RENAULT FUEGO (1982-1987)

Fans of French car design will know that the Fuego was designed by a man called Robert Opron who also styled a futuristic and much admired coupe called the Citroën SM. Unfortunately America is not home to many fans of French car design. It is, however, home to a great many people who object to driving a car that looks like an egg. And if the weird design didn't put them off, perhaps the distressingly poor acceleration would. Either that or the self-fulfilling prophesy of the name "Fuego" which meant the bulbous horror would frequently burst into flames. When it came to completely destroying a car's reputation on every front there was little else they could have done, short of paying a big man to stand at the door of every Renault showroom greeting prospective customers with a punch in the face.

VOLKSWAGEN FOX (1987–1993)

Brazil has given the world many things of note—nuts, the Lambada, a sort of minimalist ladies' hair removal technique—but this is not one of them. Instead the South American–built Fox was a sort of low-rent Rabbit which came as a sedan or, inexplicably, a two-door station wagon. Mmm, that's useful. At least North America was spared earlier iterations of this car that were fitted with the air-cooled engine from the Beetle and, as a result, made a noise like a barrel of nails being kicked around an empty warehouse. Even the revised version, a conventional 1.8-liter four-cylinder motor, sat lengthways under the hood, which is a guaranteed way to waste space in a front-wheel-drive car and something the Fox has in common with the hideous Renault Le Car. If you'd always hankered after the authentic feeling of looking like a São Paulo taxi driver then this was the car for you. Fox? Maybe they should have called it the Mongrel.

IF THIS CAR WAS...
A REAL FOX, IT'D BE
FLEA-BITTEN, MANGY,
AND INFECTED WITH RABIES.

24

DATSUN B210 (1974-1978)

In many ways the B210 had a lot going for it. Clearly not the looks, which seemed to have been created by a kid from remedial class, but it was cheap, well made, and as faithfully reliable as a Swiss watchmaker's Labrador. In conditions up to and including light nuclear warfare the little Datsun's engine would continue to start first time, every time, and that gave it a big head start over the shambling products of domestic carmakers. Rather undermining this precision engineering, however, was the marginal presence of anything resembling acceleration, handling prowess most accurately described as like trying to steer a wheelbarrow full of logs, and a tendency to go rusty just by driving within five hundred yards of a puddle. With reliability as standard, the Japanese were already well on the way to giving Detroit a thorough mauling, but as the B210 showed, it would take them a few years to really hit their stride, once they'd realized that cars last longer if you don't make the body out of the same stuff you wrap around a stick of gum.

CHRYSLER K-CAR (1981–1989)

This may have been the car that pulled Chrysler from the depths of financial trouble, but did it have to be such a weedy little griefbox? Everything about the K-car was miserable and thin, from its miserable, thin engines that gave miserable, thin performance to its miserable, thin styling, pressed from miserable, thin metal. Add together the miserable, thin total of all this miserable thinness and the whole thing was like driving around in Mary-Kate Olsen. Yeah, the K-car sold well, but then so would stale white bread in a food crisis and, with the flame of pre-fuel-crisis muscle cars well and truly extinguished by the early eighties, this was truly a time of famine. So the K-car saved Chrysler, but then Lassie saved a lot of people too, and she was still technically a bitch.

IF THIS CAR WAS...
A SAVIOR, MY GOD,
STANDARDS HAVE DROPPED
SINCE CHRIST'S TIME.

IF THIS CAR WAS...
ANY WEAKER, IT WOULDN'T
BE ABLE TO MOVE.

CHEVY CAMARO.
SHOWSTOPPING GOOD LOOKS
AND 20 EPA ESTIMATED MPG.

CHEVY'S GOT IT.
COME AND GET IT.

Chevrolet

CHEVROLET CAMARO BERLINETTA (1979)

Welcome to a strange and unpleasant parallel universe. It's a place where the imported beer is weak, Arby's is haute cuisine, and Academy Awards are repeatedly given to Pee-wee Herman. And here, in this nightmarish land, is the perfect transportation for a topsy-turvy world of mediocrity—a low-powered muscle car. Actually, despite the packaging, the Berlinetta wasn't a muscle car at all, not when it came with a V6 engine that was as powerful as a fart in a hurricane. A dead slug would have been more muscular and, just so there was no confusion, Chevy also made the Berlinetta available with fake wire-wheel hubcaps. Buy one of these and you may as well move to 1033 Loser Street, Loserville.

PONTIAC FIERO 2M4 (1984)

There are certain ways to guarantee disappointment from the get-go. Announcing a new soft drink based on beets, for example, or obtaining the financing to make a new movie version of *Hamlet* and immediately casting Steven Seagal as the lead. And when it comes to cars, you can add to that list designing a new model and basing it on the Chevrolet Chevette. Sure, they moved the engine to the middle, just like a racing car, but Pontiac engineers worked tirelessly to erase whatever excitement that might have inspired, chiefly by snuffing out anything that might pass for acceleration. And just to complete an unmemorable picture, even the Fiero's looks were slowly undermined as the plastic panels experienced severe fade-out until the color of the car became as weak as its performance.

IF THIS CAR WAS... RED WHEN YOU BOUGHT IT, YOU'D BETTER LEARN TO LIKE PINK.

20

GEO METRO
CONVERTIBLE (1990–1993)

There are various hard and fast rules of car buying. Don't buy a car that's on fire. Don't buy a car with less than four wheels. If you live in Texas don't buy a pastel-colored car or one that the previous owner has daubed with slogans such as "Ban all guns" and "Man love rools!" But wherever you live there's one rule that you should stick to above all: Don't buy a car that's smaller, and indeed less comfortable, than your shoes. Which rules out this piece of crap right away.

HYUNDAI EXCEL (1986-1989)

Great car companies rise out of one man's struggle against the odds to craft the seminal car that will forever define the passion and joy of the company that bears his name. Hyundai was not one of those companies. They were an industrial conglomerate that made stuff like ships and railroads until one day they had the bright idea of branching into cars. The result was never going to be a Porsche or a Ferrari. Or indeed very good. In fact they initially specialized in turning out miserable turds like this, sold solely because they were cheap. But then so is Boone's Farm apple wine, and you wouldn't choose that because it "goes well with the chicken."

**IF THIS CAR WAS...
ANY MORE DEPRESSING,
IT'D HAVE TO COME
WITH FREE PROZAC.**

18

MGB (1962–1980)

For some baffling reason the MGB is the darling of the classic British sports car scene. Which is odd, because it's also quite spectacular garbage. For one thing, it's based on the chassis of the Austin Cambridge, a 1950s sedan that used technology so old-fashioned it gets several mentions in the Bible. Secondly, the MGB wasn't the only thing to be built around the Cambridge chassis, because it was also the basis for the Leyland Sherpa. Which is a cargo van. So an MGB is essentially a leakier, noisier, less comfortable, and far less useful version of something once used to deliver tractor parts. In fact, there are only two things worse than actually driving an MGB: having to spend time with MGB owners as they brag about spending fifteen years stripping down the entire gearbox using only their teeth. Or having your face pushed into a lawnmower. And in that context, the lawnmower option sounds quite nice.

DODGE DAKOTA CONVERTIBLE (1989–1990)

Cars generally come in specific and well-defined genres. Compact, sports coupe, minivan, that sort of thing. Sometimes those genres cross-pollinate and there's no reason why that can't be okay. But sometimes a mix of genres is a very bad idea. Like, say, combining a pickup truck with a convertible. One question: *Why?* Memo to Dodge designers: Next time you're really really bored at work, go out and join the company softball team.

IF THIS CAR WAS… ANY DUMBER, IT'D HAVE FULL-TIME NURSING SUPERVISION.

16

IF THIS CAR WAS...
TO OFFER YOU ANYTHING,
IT WOULD BE A
NERVOUS BREAKDOWN.

CHEVROLET CITATION (1980–1985)

This was GM's first mass-produced front-wheel-drive car. So you'd think that, it being first and everything, they'd put in some extra effort, right? Well, yes, but inexplicably all that work seems to have gone into making the car crappier. One of the main problems with the Citation was that even the lightest touch on the brake pedal would cause the rear wheels to lock, which was certainly exciting. Just as, say, being shot is "exciting." Of course, experiencing the wheel lock-up problem did rather necessitate getting the car moving, and that was pretty unlikely, given that the Citation was as reliable as a Russian-made Rolex. If this was GM's idea of making a special effort for the first time, let's just be thankful they weren't first on the moon: "That's one small step for . . . Jeez! Look at the size of this place. Hey, Buzz! Cover me, man, I gotta take a whiz behind this rock . . ."

AMC GREMLIN (1970-1978)

Sometimes it's tough being a car designer. There you are, busy at work on a new and attractive body style when some dork from marketing leans over your shoulder and says, "Umm, actually this new car is meant to be a subcompact." What to do? The designs have to be submitted today and you've already promised to take your wife to her damn bridge club by seven o'clock. Oh, sure, you could stay all night rescaling your work to make the smooth, elegant lines work on a shorter vehicle. But she's been on your back all week as it is; break a promise now and she'll never let you buy that new rider mower you've had your eye on. So instead you simply take your existing design and slash off the back end. Bingo! You're out the door by 6:45 and those saps from marketing can worry about selling a car that appears to have been sawn in half. Some people say a dog can look like its owner. Well, by the same token, sometimes a car can look like its name. And a gremlin is a small ugly monster that causes trouble. Perfect.

**IF THIS CAR WAS...
A MOVIE, IT WOULD BE
"DUDE, WHERE'S THE REST
OF MY CAR?"**

14

SUZUKI SAMURAI (1987-1989)

The Samurai was sold as some sort of "fun" car, which was strange because in truth it was approximately as "fun" as falling down an elevator shaft. For one thing the performance was so leisurely that it could be outrun by a glacier. Then there was the interior space, or rather the total lack of it, which gave Samurai drivers an unwanted insight into what it would be like to become trapped in a mailbox. Finally, and most disturbingly, there was the inevitable result of the Samurai's narrow dimensions combined with its inadvisable height: It was as stable as an alcoholic on a trampoline. All in all, it would have been more fun to be attacked by an actual samurai.

CADILLAC CIMARRON
(1982–1988)

In the early 1980s, Cadillac, once a byword for peerless luxury and engineering excellence, was fast becoming associated with the more tawdry business of peddling crap. A spectacularly clumsy diesel engine fiasco and an almost equally ill-advised attempt to make a V8 that could shut down cylinders to improve gas mileage (but did so with the subtlety of a tap-dancing elephant) had given the once prestigious name an unwelcome tarnish. Something needed to be done to return it to health. Hey, what about taking the relentlessly mediocre Chevrolet Cavalier, cynically adding a few Caddy trimmings, and sending it into showrooms wearing a sticker price almost double that of the Chevy it was so clearly based on? Yeah, that ought to do it. There's no way the entire nation would immediately notice that this car was as cheap and unconvincing as a pool of vomit sprinkled with glitter. Except of course they did. As a result the Cadillac name hit a new low from which it's never recovered, and the word Cimarron has taken on a new meaning ever since. As in "Hey, buddy, your damn dog's done another Cimarron on my lawn," or "I had some bad Chinese food last night, I think I gotta take a Cimarron," or "I wasted five bucks watching *Star Wars: Episode II—Attack of the Clones*. Man, that movie was Cimarron."

IF THIS CAR WAS…
A CAVALIER, YOU'D
HAVE PAID A LOT LESS,
DUMBASS.

**IF THIS CAR WAS...
THE BEST THEY COULD DO,
NO WONDER RENAULT
DOESN'T SELL CARS IN
AMERICA ANYMORE.**

RENAULT LE CAR (1972–1985)

The Renault Le Car holds the lap record at the famous Le Mans racetrack in France. It was once the favored transport of Jack Nicholson, Frank Sinatra, and King Juan Carlos of Spain and has been depicted on high-value postage stamps in Sweden, Brazil, and the United Kingdom. In Japan the highest honor a samurai can receive is to be given a 1974 Le Car with an eight-track player in the dashboard, while in some parts of Africa it is believed that anyone who drives a Le Car is blessed with great fertility and sexual magnetism. No, wait. I was thinking of something else. The Le Car is just a big pile of crap. Sorry.

IF THIS CAR WAS...
GOOD FOR ONE THING,
IT WOULD BE
LIGHTING CIGARS.

FORD PINTO (1971–1980)

How to make an Economy Car 101. First of all, make it look cute. People like small cars that look cute. Come on, Volkswagen didn't sell a load of Bugs because they were fast, did they? Second, give it good gas mileage. It's a cheap car, no one's going to buy it if every week they have to pump it with its own weight and value in fuel. Third, make it reliable. Just because you've bought an economy car doesn't mean you should be punished, especially not when it's late, it's raining, you're lost, the damn car is pouring steam from under the hood, and how the hell did I end up in Delaware anyway? That's it, really. Looks, economy, reliability. Get those right and you'll be a shoo-in. Oh, no, wait. There's one more thing: when you're designing a new economy car it's a really good idea if you can remember to make sure that under no circumstances does it keep exploding. Did you get that last one? Hello? Hello?

10

**IF THIS CAR WAS…
TO HAVE A HOME ADDRESS,
IT'D BE UGLY AVENUE
IN THE UGLY QUARTER
OF UGLYTOWN.**

PONTIAC AZTEK (2001)

Every so often carmakers create one-off concept cars that they haul around auto shows to demonstrate what could be achieved if their designers and engineers weren't outranked by their accountants. Generally the effect is to make car buyers wish that such shiny glimpses into a bright future could be sitting in their driveways right now. Then the carmakers lock the concept cars in a big secret garage, never to be seen again, and we all feel sad. So why, of all the concept cars in all the world, did the one that made it into production have to be this one? The Pontiac Aztek—don't go entering the spelling bee any time soon, guys—isn't just an object lesson in dynamic mediocrity; it's also so hideous that simply thumbing through the sales brochure can bring on a powerful sensation of nausea. Is that a clip-on tent in the picture, or part of an elaborate disguising kit to salvage some of the driver's dignity?

SUZUKI X90 (1996–1998)

The combination of a sports coupe and an SUV. That could be a great idea. Unless of course you accidentally picked the worst bits of each and fused them together to make something as appealing as a vomit omelet. Bingo! The Suzuki X90. None of the performance of a sports car, cunningly paired with none of the ruggedness of an SUV, all wrapped in a stupid, cutesy body. If you buy a sports car you're trying to give the impression that you're dynamic and sporting. An SUV is meant to say, I'm rugged and independent and I like to wrestle bears. But if you bought a Suzuki X90 you were proudly telling the world just one thing—I am an idiot and I think I'm Barbie.

**IF THIS CAR WAS...
IN A LIST OF BAD IDEAS,
IT'D BE JUST ABOVE
NEW COKE.**

8

IF THIS CAR WAS...
THE FUTURE, WE WOULDN'T BE HERE RIGHT NOW.

CHEVROLET LUMINA APV (1990)

dashboard *n.* Believed to originate from a small shield fitted to the front of horse-drawn carriages to deflect mud kicked into the air by the animals' hooves away from the carriage occupants. "Dashboard" remains in common usage today, now referring to the forward bulkhead of a car that carries the vehicle's main controls and instruments. Or, in the case of the Chevrolet Lumina, to describe the stupid twelve-foot long lump of plastic that dominates the entire interior and takes up lots of space which, this supposedly being a minivan, might be more useful if it was filled with seats. If only the designers hadn't attempted to make a car that looked futuristic but actually ended up resembling an enormous Dustbuster with detailing work by a group of lightly trained monkeys.

CADILLAC SEVILLE (1978-1982)

As the 1970s came to a close, American automakers became mindful of a need to weather the energy crisis by making their most lavish land yachts less fuel hungry. For GM the answer came in the ominous form of a diesel engine. Not a purposefully designed motor, oh dear no, but a hasty patch-up to make an existing Oldsmobile V8 run on gasoline's less refined cousin. Then they stuffed it under the hood of their flagship lux-mobile, the Seville. The result was, predictably, appalling. Aside from the pitiful power output and woeful reliability that came from overtaxing an engine never designed to drink from the filthy black cup, the Seville diesel also belched smoke clouds so dark and noxious that starting the engine was enough to have your panicked neighbors calling the EPA. As if the rumbling, grumbling, soot-belching diseasel engine wasn't enough, GM decided to saddle the Seville with a bizarre body that started in fine Caddy style with a long, flat hood and high, proud passenger cabin and then just fizzled out into an apologetic bustle at the back. Sort of like a joke without a punch line. How apt.

IF THIS CAR WAS...
TO PROVE ONE THING, IT'S THAT SMOKING IS BAD FOR YOU.

6

CHEVROLET VEGA
(1971–1977)

Five things that dissolve more quickly than a Chevy Vega:
1. Soil
2. Orange Tang
3. Alka-Seltzer
4. Sugar in coffee
5. Errr…

IF THIS CAR WAS...
ONLY A LITTLE BIT RUSTY,
IT WAS STILL ON
THE PRODUCTION LINE.

VOLKSWAGEN BEETLE
(1945–1979)

For some reason beardy peaceniks and straggly-haired surfer dudes love the Beetle, apparently thinking it's "cool" and "alternative." Which is fine, although it does ignore the fact that it's also "garbage." What we have here is a dismal Nazi staff car with its engine in the wrong place and a list of in-built faults so long that it could fill every page in this book. Just to give you a taster, you should know that it's slow, it's noisy, it's uncomfortable, and it has such a completely pathetic heater that on cold days you'd be better off setting fire to your hair. The Beetle doesn't make you alternative and interesting at all—it simply marks you as the kind of mush-brained fool who gives pet names to inanimate objects. The only good thing about this cramped, ugly waste of perfectly good metal is that after fifty-seven years of continuous production—about fifty-five years too long—Volkswagen finally killed it off. And good riddance.

IF THIS CAR WAS...
IN YOUR KITCHEN, YOU'D STEP ON IT.

4

IF THIS CAR WAS...
ANY WORSE, YOU'D HAVE PUKED ON THIS PAGE BY NOW.

DODGE RAMPAGE
(1982–1984)

The Dodge Omni must have been in line to take a shot at being the worst car in the entire world. It was feeble, it was charmless, and it had almost no redeeming features whatsoever. At least that's what we thought. Plainly Chrysler had other ideas. They must have spent some really late nights on this one, agonizing over what they could do to make the Omni even worse. And then they cracked it—a pickup! Yes, that would be really useless. All the cloying depression and social embarrassment of owning an Omni, but with an extra side of shame courtesy of that stupid load bed out back which, this being a "compact" pickup, was about as useful as electric windows on an airplane. You've got to hand it to 'em. Not everyone could make the truly crap even crappier.

AMC PACER (1975–1980)

Oh, dear, here we go with the second funniest thing in *Wayne's World* and indeed the punch line to all car-related gags (except the ones about Pintos). You know, you could never fault AMC for trying. Wait, actually you could. Because if you're not very good at something it's probably better just to stop, which eventually they did, by going bust. But before all that there was this. A car that was meant to provide all the width, and therefore prestige, of a full-size car, with all the virtuous qualities of a compact. What it actually provided was all the embarrassment of driving a compact, with all the *extra* humiliation of driving a compact that looked like a turtle. And a hideously deformed turtle at that, because the passenger's side door was longer than the driver's. Sounds like a good idea, doesn't it? For about three seconds. Look, if it was *that* good an idea Toyota would hold the patent. But they don't, because in truth it was just another example of the kookiness that eventually caused AMC to sink. Speaking of which, has anyone ever dropped a Pacer into a river? I mean, turtles float, don't they?

IF THIS CAR WAS…
A CARTOON, IT'D BE
TEENAGE MUTANT
MANGY TURTLE.

2

IF THIS CAR WAS...
ALL YOU COULD AFFORD,
HAVE YOU CONSIDERED
PROSTITUTION?

YUGO GV (1985–1991)

The Yugo GV was proudly sold as the cheapest new car you could buy. Which is fine, as long as you remember that drowning is a pretty cheap way to die. Does that mean you'd want to do it? Nope. In fairness, drowning does sound rather more appealing than having to splutter around in this painful little Yugoslavian crap basket. The GV's basic design came from Fiat of Italy, who once made a tidy living from selling their trash to the other side of the Iron Curtain. Unfortunately the Yugoslavs thought this miserable car wasn't quite depressing enough and set about trying to ruin it. The result was slothful performance, woeful reliability, and build quality that gave the GV the permanent falling-apart-at-the-seams appearance of an abandoned shack. Still, when Yugoslavia descended into full-blown war, at least someone had the presence of mind to bomb the Yugo factory.

FORD MUSTANG II (1974)

Sequels are always a risky idea. Sometimes, if the original is so brilliant and so popular, it's best just to leave it alone rather than tarnish the name. But Ford just couldn't do that. The first-generation Mustang was already a full-fledged living legend, so how would the company keep that flame alive? By basing its replacement on the Pinto. As an unpromising start to a sequel, that would be up there with the pitch for *Driving Miss Daisy 2— Destination Spring Break*. And sure enough, the invigorating smell of crap infused every inch of the Mustang II, from its lame-o looks to a range of engines that made Bambi look mighty and strong. This being a time of gas price panic, there wasn't even the option of a V8 and, perhaps as a consequence, the '74 Mustang II didn't come saddled with anything that might be confused with acceleration. Instead it was a pitiful, unlovable, incompetent blot on the once great Mustang name. And also a really good lesson in how sequels usually turn out crap.

IF THIS CAR WAS...
ANY MORE CRAP,
IT'D HAVE FLIES
BUZZING ROUND IT.

CREDITS

Images on pages 6, 8, 9, 14, 15, 17, 21, 22, 29, 35, 37, 41, 42, 43, 47, 62, 70, 72, 73, 77, 78, 81, 86, 87 © Giles Chapman Library

Images on pages 2, 10, 11, 13, 18, 19, 25, 30, 32, 33, 34, 38, 44, 45, 46, 48, 49, 50, 51, 52, 53, 54, 55, 56, 57, 63, 64, 65, 66, 74, 82, 85, 88, 89, 90, 91, 93, 94, 96, 97, 98, 99, 100, 101, 102, 103, 104, 105, 106, 108, 109 © Richard Dredge Archive

Image on page 26 courtesy of Corey Sciuto, Tyngsboro, MA

Image on page 58 © Publications International, Ltd.

Images on pages 61 and 69 courtesy of the Detroit Public Library, National Automotive History Collection

A NOTE ON THE AUTHOR

Richard Porter is a screenwriter for the BBC's immensely popular *Top Gear* program (www.bbc.co.uk/topgear) and writes for *Evo* car magazine. Visit his spoof car news Web site at www.sniffpetrol.com.